Man Overboard:
New and Selected Poems

Michael H. Levin

Finishing Line Press
Georgetown, Kentucky

Man Overboard:
New and Selected Poems

Copyright © 2018 by Michael H. Levin
ISBN 978-1-63534-473-8 First Edition
All rights reserved under International and Pan-American Copyright Conventions. No part of this book may be reproduced in any manner whatsoever without written permission from the publisher, except in the case of brief quotations embodied in critical articles and reviews.

ACKNOWLEDGMENTS

Versions of some of these poems originally appeared as follows:

"Human Rights" and "Man Overboard," in *Poetica Magazine* (2016)
"Note to the Queen of the Night," in *Poem of the Week* (Poetica Publishing, 10 August 2015) (on line)
"Brief Encounter" and "Stone Steps," in *The Federal Poet* (2016, 2017)
"Months After," in *Poet Lore* (1979)

Publisher: Leah Maines
Editor: Christen Kincaid
Cover Art: Paul Fleet/Shutterstock.com
Author Photo: Public Domain
Cover Design: Elizabeth Maines McCleavy

Printed in the USA on acid-free paper.
Order online: www.finishinglinepress.com
　　　　　also available on amazon.com

　　　　　　　　Author inquiries and mail orders:
　　　　　　　　　　Finishing Line Press
　　　　　　　　　　　P. O. Box 1626
　　　　　　　　　Georgetown, Kentucky 40324
　　　　　　　　　　　　U. S. A.

Table of Contents

Almost a Volcano 1
Brief Encounter... 3
Burning 4
Crocodile Tears 5
Five A.M. in the E.R. 6
Fourth Hour of the Amduat.. 7
Guide to Pompeii... 8
Hitler Shaves 9
Human Rights.. 10
It's Not about Sex 11
Late Dive... 12
Lysol Dreams.. 13
Man Overboard 14
Mephistopheles by Night.. 15
Months After.. 16
National Museum of African-American History............ 18
Norma Jean.. 19
Note, to the Queen of the Night 20
Notes on The Winter's Tale... 21
Our Sixties.. 22
Self-Portrait, With Secrets.. 23
Stone Steps, Merton College Oxford 25
Study in Blue and Green... 26
Summers Near Stowe 27
The Gods Come Out... 28
The Royal Tombs of Ur 29
The Typist 30
Wannsee 31
All Poems Are Protests... 32

*To Caden and Ben-O
Grandsons; Renewers*

ALMOST A VOLCANO
(Osorno, Puerto Varas, 2017)

Before the clouds closed
almost we saw the volcano
rising like Fuji
from turquoise waves.

Before the rains came
nearly we glimpsed that
improbable fusion
of stillness and consuming heat,

an ice thorn thrust
from the spine of the Andes
by the pressure of liquid stone
on immense granite glissades.

Before the moon set
it sparkled off swords of snow
shafting down, points towards
the sleeping harbor's heart

where solitary couples
stumbled home along the costanera
as the wildness of Chile gathered
above them like thunderheads,

savage as pumas on hunting grounds,
piling up, dark with electric shocks
and the thin bird-call voices
of the disappeared.

We should kill them all
our guide said later on a trek
through lupines and fire-bush
about tribes asserting lost rights,

they just cause trouble for
all of us—*todos Chile,*
meaning iron Chile, that land
compressed and implacable

as glaciers which grind
in one direction, crushing
dissent. But the condors
remained untroubled, cruising

indifferent thermals
on big-fingered spans.
Black scarabs mated on sun-warmed trails.

Lapwings too were indifferent,
patrolling their borders
with monochrome cries.

Before the clouds closed
almost we saw the volcano:

a mirage of perfection
above curled turquoise waves.

BRIEF ENCOUNTER

James O'Malley, suit-and-tied,
even by a white sand beach,
sat well-starched with phone surfside
shooting cuffs (the world in reach)

calling clients each by each
punching buttons with aplomb
stuffing voice-mails with stiff speech.
Alas, they none of them were home:

they spied his number and preferred
a root canal or broken thumbs
to more whereases and whereofs
or pendent clauses framed by "such"

and laid their bright devices down,
spooning up crème fraiche with peach.
Along the shore then came a Fool
with tangled hair and lurching gait

who gestured with unfocused gaze
(drunk or crazed could not be told)
and looked upon O'Malley's face
then squatted there and dropped a turd

and grinned disjointedly; and bowed
and went his way. Leaving our James
agape at blasted rules: displeased
at that disorderly brief phase.

Uneasy who was properly the fool.
Uncertain if he heard
(or if he could) faint birdsong
from a distant golden wood.

BURNING
(1953: Plaquemines Parish, during the smallpox)

Loose bales slumped like home folks
on a veranda leak rolled skirts
and trousers on October ground.
Among blond stover, bras
rear upright, their cones
catching low sun.

Bill Cor who runs the dozer
watching them fed to the drum
incinerators shifts
his chaw nervously, scratches
gray stubble, fends off their
retention of shape.

Still they burn down,
popping and melting.
Black smoke tails east.
The crew wears masks
and rubber gloves
filmed with sweat.

Seizing and pitching
they mimic plague times.
Odd how these objects insist
on themselves, coil into the same
flexed knees, hitched shoulders.
Like Shakespearean cloaks

they know their roles
better than actors: carbonize
in character before
collapsing to ash.
Collapsing, collapsing.
Collapsing to ash.

CROCODILE TEARS
(For N. L., 1877-1967)

That last day with
my father's Pop, he stood
by his assisted living
door—a short thick dark
mustachioed form, squeeze
bag just visible, a tear
on one swarthy leather cheek.

Why tears from that
stern man (a crocodile
who barely smiled), I wonder
now. For him—the long Carpathian
journey through chipped pushcarts to
American ease, near close?
The family splintered into warring

states beyond repair?
His children making separate
visits, not to meet?
Or was it me, then twenty
in a blaze of youth
that might go on to crystallize
in shapes unseen. What fixed

that moment was his lifelong
aura of cigar; mixed whiffs
of urine and mopped antiseptic
floor; the trick he liked to play
with narrow jars that would not
let small fists out, fat with coins.
And in that moment I moved

helplessly to hug him, surprised
how small the ogre was.
I swear he pressed his bullet
head against my chest.
The summer curtains stirred. Then
we—and he (I thought)—
were gone.

FIVE A.M. IN THE E.R.

Bins of stained sheets
line the corridor. Banked phones
bleep klingon mating calls. Nearby
half-interviews; a harried white-shoe squeak.
My son, so loved for his troubles, lies
in a neck brace, blood on his cheek,
in his hair, beneath his cuticles.
It's Halloween, though

his exploded face is no disguise.
Who put him here's unknown.
I pace, recalling his spotlight grin
and what they'd do where Clint comes from.
Time oozes like antifreeze
in a Midwest-winter radiator.

FOURTH HOUR OF THE AMDUAT
(Burial Chamber of Thutmose III, Valley of the Kings)

> *With the [Soul's] fourth hour in the Underworld, the fertile landscape stops abruptly, giving way to the desert of Ro-setau, a barren kingdom populated with serpents [whose] sinister mobility is emphasized with legs and wings . . . A zigzag path runs through this hour region, full of fire and repeatedly blocked by doors. The darkness is so deep that the sun god is unable to recognize the inhabitants . . . But the light needs the darkness to be able to renew itself.*
> —Erik Hornung, "Exploring the [Pharoahs'] Beyond"

Now Water is Sand, the realm
of Sokar, consort of Sakhmet, Mistress
of Fear. It grates like salt along the
baking natron plain.   Bright air turns dark,
still as the sunset hush
when even insects pause.
At the hour's black center
bird-headed Thoth holds up
the Solar Eye.

                       Night after night
night swallows the Sun.   How comforting
to know the spells that bind us to
that journey: that swallow
the terrors of seeing and not
seeing, the chaos
of a blind weird wriggling
afterworld. That re-stitch the body
triumphant, with each leap of
resurrecting dawn.

GUIDE TO POMPEII

Unearthing this city
Victorian diggers hacked
its pink murals, battered
with picks rose
phallic appliqués
though Mysteries
said "Psalms" to them,
unfit to sense
that painted prayers
draped frenzy.

Traveler, note well:
in every villa's light
an echoed same—the musk
of fresh-turned soil,
an alien strain.
Bright frescoed gods
gaze down, eternal,
strange: knot-veined
embodiments
of appetite.

HITLER SHAVES
(1925)

The black eye dead as a shark's
flickers to life across the plumb-line
creases cornering his mouth,
the bad teeth, the hated cowlick
always verging out of control.

Bent over the washstand
he regards himself coldly
in a small square mirror. The room's
cold too for a round-shouldered guy
who sucks in his breath to seem tall.

Will is the thing—hard lodestone
of repressed desire. The eye
turns searchlight: pinpoint, brilliant.
The air clamors with klaxons
that only he hears.

Steam floats from brushed foam in its bleached
balsam cup. The straight stropped razor
weights his hand, balancing breakfast
and blood. Strange thrill, to test it
with a crookéd thumb. Clean steel,

sharp and undoubtful. It rings on
porcelain like a mess bell. Sun fades behind
broken clouds. *Stahl passend ist*,
he murmurs. *Meist passend.*
Steel is good.

HUMAN RIGHTS

Even the crippled, the cringing,
the beggars squatting cross-legged
among balls of dung along
the road, squeezed forth by
shanty walls, have leave to sink
to dappled chairs on public grass;
inhale spring air; accept soft
sunbeams' kind massage.

                                    We are
those forms behind the wire—dispersed stray
point-men in an ancient war, two
breaths from barbed despair. If
fortune smiles, beware: the smile
is thin. Cascading disappointments
are foreshadowed there.

IT'S NOT ABOUT SEX
        (*Liaisons Dangereuses:* Valmont to Merteuil, 1782)

I must insist on that—
no ravenous twined hunger
riving me; no licks or bites,
lace bonds or kitten cries.
It's dialogue I crave, the words
an inlaid portrait of your wily
female soul: sleek as a cobra
and as sinuous, inhabiting
starched customs and constricted
ways—until you rise, spreading your hood.

Don't fix me with your tawny eyes
suggesting innocence,
or dip dark lashes in pretended
modesty. I know too well
the layers that slide beneath
your golden skin, your homing scent
for prey. Since we were children
on that far estate, examining with
sheer delight forbidden parts,
communion has been naked,

diamond-hard. Now Paris calls,
all dominations catechized.
We will be partners in a novel
power game and set our traps
for those who, trusting beauty,
follow urgings into nets they
cannot see. Only do not consult
me on cool mornings when the sun
outlines your limbs; or twilights
when I struggle to resist

that faintly pulsing hollow
in your neck. Desire matured
takes forms the virtuous would flee:
a ceaseless swallowing,
engulfing lesser wills with slow
extruded fire.

LATE DIVE

How difficult are phantoms to disclaim.

I drop through layers,
parting the water column.
Pale fishes, luminous eels
curl by, inspecting
incuriously. Down

and down further, light dwindles,
my body gives up its gravity:
elastic, compressed,
a descending accordion.
Breath booms and rumbles

rolling like tympani.
Bottomed at last
the roiled ground of dreams
slowly disrobes itself—murky
striptease of disclosure:

a rough-edged reef range
rapt with arms waving
bile-green and poisonous;
opiate seascape
where speech clots, touch wounds.

How long before
that distant sky's regained
where osprey spiral
air on sunstruck wings?

How difficult, our phantoms to disclaim.

LYSOL DREAMS

It's ten a.m.
She swabs latrines.
The leavings of strange others
do not match her dreams.
Their discards left behind
(gelatinous room-service trays)
could feed the bird-boned squads
of children in San Salvador
she fled.

By noon she's done
with what her vacuum
suctions up. She snaps ranked beds
in place, inhaling whiffs of fresh
high-count Egyptian cotton sheets;
between each corner-fold, breathes deep
as though the bleach fumes
just released were blue sky
valley air.

At four her quota
is complete. She closets
up her cart—its mop, wipes,
color-coded sprays—
together with desire. Then
thrusts her key out, dagger-wise.
There's no return, and no one
to attack. She shrugs, then
faintly smiles, and turns
her back.

MAN OVERBOARD
(C.G.R., b. Fort Atkinson, d. 2004)

Dark head bobbing in a chevron wake
disconnected as the space surged
you slipped through the O
of our grasp.

Cool as Wisconsin, you forgot
safe dreams are toxic, that fear is how we fly:
stood off, maneuvering. We scan your log now
seeking its theme.

Cold virtues are an ancient curse—
they reek of Artemis and Mimë.
To wall off one's heart with denial, is to
starve the self away.

Our saving grace is to open
like glories; for openness is all
the earth we have, we dots on the
sliding gray plates

of a following sea.

MEPHISTOPHELES BY NIGHT

It is the weariness
that weighs on me:
this slacked anticipation
denser than lead.
The hunter's thrill
displaced by empty airs.
Where I rose to the scent
like a wolfhound,
stretching elastic limbs,
a mannerist remains:
well-brushed, white suit,
red boutonnière displayed—
the best-dressed of the lot still.
All thirst boiled off. Uncoiled.

Just once from all my offers
would have quite sufficed—
to see a hesitation, if not horrors
to defy. But no: they snap up
each barbed bargain
from half-baited lines.
What triumph's left
in setting out?
His ultimate revenge:
that I, even I,
chief fallen angel, lie here,
prostrate and perilous
poisoned by hope

MONTHS AFTER
(For C.M.G.)

What I remember
is the color red—red hair
red cheeks, your face
a mirrored Ireland still
through masks of kohl and Fabergé;
that lobster skin when
characteristically
in the Caribbean
you slandered pink, declared
for brown, stretched
your long arms to the sun
and swung for hours
in hammocked splendor, poached
like a glamorous egg.

I have heard your sisters sing
passing in flocks or going home
have seen their diffident
shy loveliness
but not that intensity
within which friendship bloomed
as in a greenhouse, the lush
silk richness of camellias

and wonder now
if your bright dresses
racked in their lightless closet rows
like cardboard flowers waiting
to be born, shimmied a last time,
shaped their slack threads
to your form once more,
ready as always to embrace the moment,
before they were thrown out
or given away.

Thinking of that, and how
memory is merciless
discarding like gamblers
what it cannot use,
and your desperate, fluid, lavish,
impassioned grace, reduced now
to a fan of photographs
I re-read your obituary

feeling you drift
like its yellowed
curlicue: last leaves
on a slow
November
wind.

NATIONAL MUSEUM OF AFRICAN-AMERICAN HISTORY
(District of Columbia: Fall 2016)

This is the lumbar region
of the world, a knotted spine
whose segments broadcast pain.
The Middle Passage still throws
shadows here: night sweats
still cramped by unseen chains.

Somehow by bright
church hats or gospel tunes
through gnarled blind
passages they made a way,
in time laid paths where there were
none; left Egypt's blank despair behind.

Yet hauled loads and hewed
wood still caw. O country, you
know well first sin. Our hooded
serpent wakes, then rises ring-
side from hoed rows of cotton
bolls again. No cure for snakes

can last: we're bound
winged angel to its demon
in a whole. Though dignity
acknowledged might
someday contain this one
sciatica of soul.

NORMA JEAN
    (Laguna, 1951)

The sky regards the beach
regards these men regarding
the bathing-suited girl
in stacked heels, and her boobs.
That's me. It's L.A. hot.

My body was the wing
to fly away, but still I'm
looking in. They crowd and crush,
flicking forked lids,
hungry for soft flesh welling

from halter lines. I wave
and laugh and bounce; oblige.
They are the face of nothing.
Nothing can fill me up.

NOTE, TO THE QUEEN OF THE NIGHT
(Magic Flute, Metropolitan Opera, 2014)

I want to know
as this last of so many curtains
falls on spangled shapes; pin spots; bright moon
shafts piercing velvet dark—why is it you

who gets the song: that dazzling string
of glorious a capella pearls, flung
at the hall like a great expanding necklace
radiant with power, whose

words reek murderous revenge?
The sun may win, dissolving your deep night
yet it's your doubled theme that stays.
Beneath the mumbo-jumbo of the play

the score speaks clear— I want to know
if you suspect (as you press on in your
ferocious quest, soaring past lunar notes
to that black B) the gift is retrograde:

all surfaces deceive. To be fulfilled
a self transcending self must be achieved.

NOTES ON *THE WINTER'S TALE*

Suppose it were true.
Was it worth it:

those jealous swirls
the oracles cut raging down

that cataract of griefs
scattering the crowd like change

the two-hour prelude meant
to bring us to a close

where blindness, spent,
gets resurrection as its recompense?

Hermione's unshrived lament,
Pérdita lost, refound:

their radiant innocence
whispers a dark

female resilience—
Antigonus still eaten by his bear,

Pauline remarried leaves
no broken circle there.

OUR SIXTIES
(Kent Island MD: a party)

Twist and shout friends
you look quite fine;
in tonight's back beat
no gray or loose flanks
show. Survivors
of brown rice, lies
and chemo, flushed
as Watteaus and stretched
down pine floors in
dance-dazed space
like murals in a mastaba,
you are as you were—
husked kernels of brightness,
a slow smooth swirl extending,
till the sedge at the skyline
turns salmon. Until
the music dies.

SELF-PORTRAIT, WITH SECRETS
(After Ashbery)

On the rear reflected wall
an oak-framed horseman canters
with a falcon on his fist,
conveying no more meaning
than this crop-haired countenance
gazing back calmly with a
slivered smile above the hand
that loosely grasps a loaded
brush or pen—I can't tell which.

Each object is reversed, of course.
His splattered mirror does its
usual dance. The painted rider
hurtles left not right; our subject's
pink-veined wattles (caught in the
wake of motion beneath ice-blue eyes)
tilt yet another way. Perhaps
that framed ensemble just was bought—
a backyard sale. Perhaps

the hawk reminds him of some
savage pride subdued, or—glaring
past furzy slopes that drumming hoofbeats clear—
recaptures appetite not sanded smooth
by age. Perhaps this play of light
along his shaven jaw is
merely play—a flourish technical
and sure, recounting pleasure
in acrylic swirl, no more.

All's surface here, intently
focused upon planes of cheek
and jowl within vague radiant space.
I hear the critics distantly

converse, debating background rhythms
versus foreground tour de force.

What isn't captured's where
his life might prowl, investing
artifice with predatory fire.

Betrayals don't seem shadowed
in that barely-wrinkled brow
or disappointments early
and mid-race, or struggles shuttered
by his tight-lipped mouth; or necessary
lies. Or seasons of exhaustion
when, like jellyfish, we settle
in our tanks, bells upside down.

Yet those who've tasted even
at the margins know the
texture of the game.
Each birth's—first—fear of sorrow—
then a clenched consuming drive.
The live ones rest on drained relief
suspended out of time. Without that
edge of terror no slick mannerist
however arrogant or suave
can wear the crown.

STONE STEPS, MERTON COLLEGE OXFORD
(To Nevill Coghill my teacher)

Risers a masonry class:
plumb perfect for six hundred years.
At their turn by the landing an
arch glows, yellow with sun. My dropped
coin rings, silver-belled.

I leapt these stairs in spring then
before grapes and cheese, sprawled picnics,
suppers drenched in Bordeaux. Before
births, breached knees, the fall. Now
ballast slows me. Yet

cresting this climb still I see you:
a cave bear shambling, crag-browed,
awkward as condors, all
tweed knobs and angles. You loom
like an oak; ask

does Lear curse the storm
though we both know curses are
sideshows. Acceptance, acceptance
matters—the proud soaked head erect,
wind stooped over,

rattling with rain. It's balance
that's kingly; and the long silent quest
when we wrestled as equals
for essence. When I leafed out, a
green willow by water,

found footed order. Found judgment
was rooted in love.

STUDY IN BLUE AND GREEN
(Visiting my mother-in-law, age 94)

An azure Florida sky
hypnotic as the ripples
of this cove on which I float

her celadon eye
where light flicks briefly
like mosquito wings.

Survived five countries
now that fierce will seeps,
a slow choked stream.

Amphibious, I enter
her Cretaceous time
that creeps like syrup

join her, salt-glazed,
half asleep.

SUMMERS NEAR STOWE
(Vermont, 1950s)

Before these hills
grew downhill spas
half-timbered chalets
gated estates for hedge fund
refugees, the crop was farm boys:
thick-legged guys with hard palms
and acne, sanded by winter,
who skied to four-room schools from need.

We played them in the county
Babe Ruth League: a summer camp
against town teams; new store-bought
outfits versus pick-me-ups. Their
infields pegged throws round the horn in
jeans. Those games meant gritted
slides, dodged curves, sharp flying spikes.
Something elusive made them fierce

that sprung lashed drives, snapped
change-ups hurled for hours at barns.
As I recall we never won,
too innocent to deal with
what was caged. For us it was
just ball. We left on schedule
for cold swims, clay tennis courts.
I wondered why they couldn't

join the dare-me plunges to our
spring-fed pool. But strangeness
closed this off in hand-slaps
that avoided eyes. Seeing comes later—
late. Too late to cross old tribal lines
or enter into modes of being
that now reside in ankle-scars
from blocking old home plates.

THE GODS COME OUT
We shot the scenes at dusk, when the gods come out.
—Alejandro Iñáritu, Director, *The Revenant (2015)*

At dusk the gods emerge—
erect, gray-eyed; striding
horizons where red sun
lines fade. Absorbed in god
things and opaquely cloaked
they gaze beyond; adjust
their sandals, soon move on.

Unmarred by human pain
they seldom answer letters
or respond to pleas. Not
granting that it's mortal lives
which justify bronze pride
they hike their mortgaged robes
incline fine modeled heads

and coolly glide. By
grace of us survive.

THE ROYAL TOMBS OF UR
(Traveling exhibit, 1999)

Consorts still hold silver spears;
dames spoon out haunch to haunch
in abacus rows, jostling each other,
pale calcite cups at hand,
last toast to their Own,
the dead Queen.

Treasure boils up like lava
from the mud—gold brooches, pins,
slim diadems with hammered leaves;
an ivory goat nibbling acanthus seeds.
The beaded lapis cape that jangled
when She strode.

Did each drink willingly—choke down
that pyroclastic potion with a smile?
Or was choice hesitant;
iron law; a priestly designation
like a roll call?

Four thousand years
have not erased
the hilts of their daggers.

The rope of our past is long:
is tie; is noose:
they were necessary deaths.
O city of Abraham
your cradle stands
on doubtful ground,
a garden fertilized
with scapulas and blood.

The mouths of these graves
mouth screams.

THE TYPIST
(Second gunner, Sherman M-4: February 1945, past the Rhine)

They shipped me straight from
typing school, shuffling file cards
the Army way: without a clue.
I knew to change two-color
ribbons, not boxed ammo belts.

Strapped in this metal can
five guys who haven't washed for weeks
crush bodies in cold mud
clank on. The stench inside and out
is not to be believed: latrines
and cordite; sweat, burned eaves,
blue gangrene, diesel fumes.

I read in Revelations
where the seal splits and that Rider
gallops out. He rides with us,
we're him—a three-horned beast
that spreads destruction on the land.
No end to days—I'm at my desk,
clamped in a bucking bolted seat,
typing away at sixty rounds
per squeeze. Like keystrokes
punching onionskin

I hammer out the scene.

WANNSEE

> *On 20 January 1942 a fateful meeting of high Nazi officials was held in the [elegant] Minoux villa by the Wannsee waterside . . . on the organized deportation and murder of Jews in the occupied areas of Poland and Eastern Europe.*
> —Website, House of the Wannsee Conference, Berlin

The windows are white-crossed,
reflecting old salvations.
Beyond stone urns that furnish
such gardens the lake
sighs quietly; subsides to
chrome steel under failing light.

A blind king
wandering outside would find
no children seeking blessing
entered from stage left—just paths
prepared for exits. Dim figures
glide behind the foggy glass,

flattened by optics
and self-assurance.
The arrogance of lists has
conquered death, it seems, and bent
all terror to its will.

The king inclines his matted
head. He knows what must
be earned by pain, who finally
will burn. For some time
till this cycle runs
he won't return.

ALL POEMS ARE PROTESTS,

subversive as moles that spade
ten feet per hour through virgin
earth, leaving strange humps and sunken trails

we stumble on. Unruly as bees
that hive their stubborn course
from bloom to bloom. Razored as tools

that rhythmically drive straight, producing
mortised joints from shavings.
Where richness stuns distracted minds

and spreads its spangled quilt, no
riot gear or tumbril chants
need advertise. In poems

the moment only calls—a sudden
yearning glimpsed through others' eyes—
and in that call all arguments

against routine are crystallized.

Mike Levin has long juggled writing with professional and family demands. His journalism has appeared in the *Wall Street Journal, New York Times, Washington Post, Harvard Magazine, Pennsylvania Gazette* and other periodicals. His critical articles have appeared in (e.g.) *Asides* (Shakespeare Theatre), *Studies in English Literature* (Tulane) and *Renascence* (Marquette). His poetry has appeared in *Wisconsin Review, Poet Lore, Midstream, Poetica, Martha's Vineyard Writing, Adirondack Review, The Federal Poet* and numerous other journals. He received two American Independent Writers awards for best published poem (2003, 2008) and was cited in the *Writer's Digest* (2013, 2015) and *Anna D. Rosenberg* (2015, 2016) annual poetry competitions. His work has been published in anthologies including *Joys of the Table: An Anthology of Culinary Verse* (Richer Resources, 2015), *Poets Are Present* (Shakespeare Theatre Company, 2015) and *Such an Ugly Time* (Rat's Ass Review, 2017). His chapbook *Watered Colors* (Poetica, 2014) was described by *Harvard Magazine* as "a debut collection [rich in] emotional imagery," and by the Washington Independent Review of Books as "showing poetry makes us alive as we can be."

Mike spent almost two decades in federal government as a lawyer, policy expert and executive with the Environmental Protection Agency and other agencies, in the Carter White House, and as Congressional Fellow to Hon. Andrew Maguire (D-NJ) and the late Sen. Edward M. Kennedy (D-MA). He then was in private practice at national law firms before founding his own law firm and transitioning to financial advice and structuring renewable energy projects. He currently is an environmental / transactions lawyer and solar energy developer based in Washington DC and Menemsha (Martha's Vineyard) MA.

Mike holds honors degrees from the University of Pennsylvania and Harvard Law School and an M.Litt. in English Language and Literature (concentration: theatre) from Oxford University, where he was a University of Pennsylvania Thouron Fellow and the last graduate student of Gresham Professor Nevill Coghill—playwright, critic, translator of Chaucer's *Canterbury Tales,* author (among other books) of *Shakespeare's Professional Skills,* and part of the Oxford Inklings group whose members included J.R.R. Tolkien and C.S. Lewis.

www.ingramcontent.com/pod-product-compliance
Lightning Source LLC
LaVergne TN
LVHW041602070426
835507LV00011B/1259